B.L.   5.4

Pts.   0.5

101 Facts About
PETS
101 Facts About

101 FACTS ABOUT

GUINEA PIGS

Please visit our web site at: www.garethstevens.com
For a free color catalog describing Gareth Stevens Publishing's list of high-quality
books and multimedia programs, call 1-800-542-2595 (USA) or 1-800-461-9120
(Canada). Gareth Stevens Publishing's Fax: (414) 332-3567.

Library of Congress Cataloging-in-Publication Data

Barnes, Julia, 1955-
101 facts about guinea pigs / Julia Barnes.
p. cm. — (101 facts about pets)
Includes bibliographical references and index.
ISBN 0-8368-2887-9 (lib. bdg.)
1. Guinea pigs as pets—Miscellanea—Juvenile literature.   2. Guinea pigs as
pets—Behavior—Miscellanea—Juvenile literature.   [1. Guinea pigs—Miscellanea.
2. Guinea pigs as pets—Miscellanea.]   I. Title: One hundred one facts about
guinea pigs.   II. Title.   III. Series.
SF459.G9B375   2001
636.9'3592—dc21   2001031151

This North American edition first published in 2001 by
Gareth Stevens Publishing
A World Almanac Education Group Company
330 West Olive Street, Suite 100
Milwaukee, WI 53212 USA

This U.S. edition © 2001 by Gareth Stevens, Inc. Original edition © 2001 by Ringpress Books
Limited. First published by Ringpress Books Limited, P.O. Box 8, Lydney, Gloucestershire,
GL15 4YN, United Kingdom. Additional end matter © 2001 by Gareth Stevens, Inc.

Ringpress Series Editor: Claire Horton-Bussey
Ringpress Designer: Sara Howell
Gareth Stevens Editor: Heidi Sjostrom

Printed in Hong Kong through Printworks Int. Ltd.

1 2 3 4 5 6 7 8 9 05 04 03 02 01

101 FACTS ABOUT

GUINEA PIGS

Julia Barnes

Gareth Stevens Publishing
A WORLD ALMANAC EDUCATION GROUP COMPANY

2 Guinea pigs come from South America, where they have lived for thousands, or possibly millions, of years. In the wild, they live in family groups called colonies.

3 Wild guinea pigs make their homes in spaces between rocks or in burrows that other small animals have left behind. They eat grass and other plants and drink very little water.

1 Guinea pigs are very popular pets. They are small and gentle, they like people, and they hardly ever bite or scratch.

4 Guinea pigs were highly valued by the **Incas** who lived in Peru – but not as pets. The Incas used guinea pigs for food and religious sacrifices.

5 Today, some guinea pigs still run wild in Peru, but most are kept as pets – in many countries.

6 Nobody knows how guinea pigs got their name. They are not related to pigs, but, when you see a guinea pig trot or hear it squeal, it might remind you of a pig!

7 Guinea pigs are also known as **cavies**. Breeders and other experts prefer to use this name.

8 Animals are divided into groups that have similar habits and body structures. Guinea pigs belong to the **rodent** group, along with mice, rats, gerbils, hamsters, porcupines, and chinchillas.

9 Although these rodents might appear different, they all have teeth that grow all the time, so they are all animals that **gnaw**.

10 The closest relatives of guinea pigs are nutria rats, porcupines, and chinchillas, all of which come from South America, Central America, and the Caribbean.

11 Guinea pigs usually live to be about five years old, but some live much longer.

12 The oldest guinea pig on record was Snowball, a pet guinea pig in Nottinghamshire, England. Snowball died in February 1979 at the grand old age of 14 years and 10 months.

16 Some people like to keep rabbits and guinea pigs together, but guinea pigs are shy, and rabbits sometimes bully them. A female rabbit that is a small breed might be a good companion for a guinea pig, but only if the two animals are put together at a young age.

13 Adult females, called sows, weigh up to 2 pounds (900 grams).

14 Adult males, called boars, weigh slightly more than females.

15 Guinea pigs like to live in small groups. Keeping two or three sows together is best. Boars that are kept together often fight.

17 Buy your guinea pig at a good pet store that has an experienced staff to give you advice.

18 Do not buy a guinea pig that looks sickly just because you feel sorry for it. You could end up with a lot of sadness and expense trying to make it well.

19 Choose a guinea pig that is about six weeks old. With gentle handling, a young guinea pig will be easy to tame.

20 A healthy guinea pig is lively and curious. The picture below shows you some things to check for before buying one.

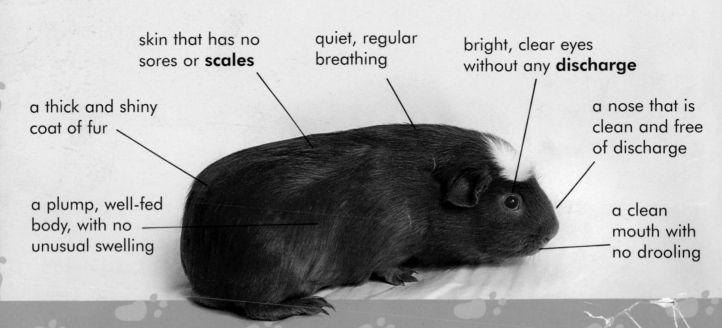

skin that has no sores or **scales**

quiet, regular breathing

bright, clear eyes without any **discharge**

a thick and shiny coat of fur

a nose that is clean and free of discharge

a plump, well-fed body, with no unusual swelling

a clean mouth with no drooling

21 Also, before you buy, ask an expert to tell you whether the guinea pig you want is a boar or a sow.

22 Three kinds of guinea pigs are the most common:
- Smooth-haired **breeds**, such as the American varieties, have short hair that lies flat.
- Long-haired breeds, such as Peruvians, have long, trailing hair that is parted down the back.
- Abyssinians (right) have a rough coat of fur that has circular patterns, called whorls or rosettes, on it.

23 Most pet stores sell **crossbred** guinea pigs, which make ideal pets. If you want guinea pigs for showing, you should buy **purebred** guinea pigs. To find purebreds you will probably have to go to a special breeder.

24 Special breeding programs have produced guinea pigs with some unusual types of coats. A Rex has short, thick, wool-like fur that stands straight up, like velvet. A Satin has fine, dense, short fur that is silky and shiny.

▲ Satin Cream

▲ silver and white Agouti Rex

25 Guinea pigs come in a range of colors and markings. A guinea pig that is all one color is a "self" type. With two or more colors, it is a "marked" type.

26 Guinea pigs with distinct coat patterns include Agoutis, with two or more bands of color on each hair; Dalmatians, with white

◀ spotted
Dalmatian

bodies and black heads and spots; Tortoiseshells, with blocks of red and black fur; Dutch, with a white "saddle" and **blaze**; and Himalayans, with a light-colored body and markings like a Siamese cat.

27 Other guinea pig varieties include the crested breeds, which are self types with a single rosette, or crest, of a different color in the center of the head.

28 Silkies, or Shelties, are a long-haired breed, like Peruvians, except that their long, soft hair does not cover the face or part over the back.

29 All purebred guinea pigs in shows are judged by Breed Standards that describe the perfect size, shape, color, and type of coat for each variety.

▲ Dutch Red

30 A smooth-haired guinea pig might be the best choice for your first pet guinea pig. They are good-natured and do not need much grooming.

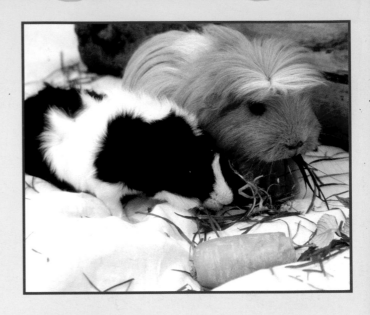

31 Most guinea pigs are hardy, or strong, but they can get sick, so you should find a **veterinarian** in your area who has experience treating guinea pigs.

32 In cold weather, guinea pigs are not as tough as rabbits. If yours lives outdoors, make sure you bring it inside for the winter.

33 Do not, however, keep your guinea pig in a garage. The fumes from a car could kill it.

34 A **hutch** for your guinea pig should be at least 3 feet (1 meter) wide, 2 feet (0.6 m) deep, and 1½ feet (0.5 m) high.

35 To protect your pet from drafts, the hutch should be raised off the ground on legs at least 9 inches (23 centimeters) long.

36 The hutch must have strong door latches or fasteners to keep your guinea pig from getting out and enemies, such as dogs and cats, from getting in.

37 The front of the hutch should have a screen or wire mesh covering with small openings, so mice and rats cannot get inside.

38 A hutch could have many different designs. The picture below shows some basic features that will keep your guinea pig safe and comfortable.

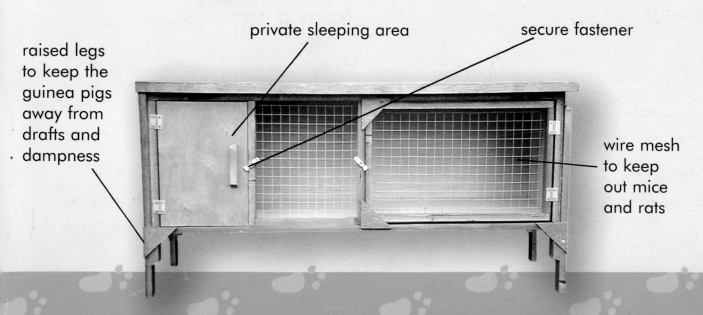

private sleeping area

secure fastener

raised legs to keep the guinea pigs away from drafts and dampness

wire mesh to keep out mice and rats

39 If your guinea pig lives indoors in a cage, keep the cage in a quiet place. Put an empty box inside the cage so your pet will have a private area.

40 Try to keep your guinea pig away from televisions and radios. It has very sensitive hearing and can be upset by loud noises or high-pitched sounds.

41 When you keep your guinea pig in a cage indoors, you have to be sure it gets enough exercise. You can make an exercise run out of a shallow box lined with wood shavings. It should be 12 feet (3.5 m) square for up to three guinea pigs.

42 Some owners allow their guinea pigs to run free in a small area of the house. Be sure this area is completely safe, with no electrical cords or other dangers. Remember, guinea pigs love to gnaw, so protect any wooden furniture.

43 Watch your guinea pig closely when it is out of its cage. Guinea pigs are quick to find hiding places that might be hard for you to reach.

44 Guinea pigs can be trained, like a cat, to use a litter box. If you keep the guinea pig in a small area where it can easily get at the litter box, it should start using the box, but do not get angry with your pet if it makes a mistake.

45 A guinea pig needs plenty of bedding on the floor of its cage to keep warm.

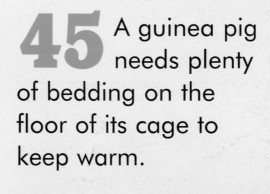

46 The best bedding for your guinea pig is wood shavings with a layer of hay over them. Do not use straw. It has sharp ends.

47 A guinea pig needs fresh water at all times. The best way to provide it is to attach a special water bottle to the side of your pet's hutch or cage.

48 A guinea pig likes to run across its food dish and throw food around. Use a heavy bowl with a wide base so it will not tip over.

49 Unlike many other rodents, guinea pigs do not play with toys. They do, however, like to have places to hide. If you cut some holes in a sturdy cardboard box, you can watch your guinea pig scurry in and out.

50 With some pieces of 4-inch (10-cm) plastic pipe, you can make tunnels that could lead to a secret food supply! Your pet will love investigating.

51 In summer, guinea pigs enjoy being outdoors to exercise and eat grass, so make sure your guinea pig has an exercise run. Part of the run must be in the shade, and be sure to attach a water bottle.

52 Guinea pigs like to sunbathe, too, but they might overdo it. White animals get sunburned easily, especially on their ears. The best time to take your guinea pig outside is early morning or late afternoon, when the sun is not so hot.

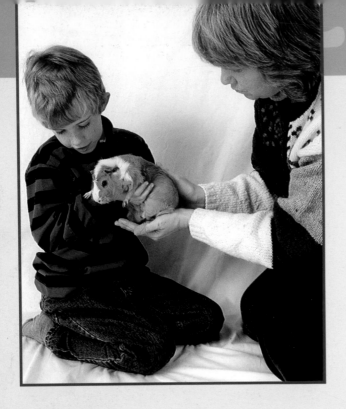

newcomer. Put lots of food in an exercise run and let the guinea pigs eat together. Make sure the other guinea pigs accept the new arrival before you put them all in the same sleeping area.

53 Do not handle your pet guinea pig too much when you first bring it home. Give it a chance to explore its new surroundings and get used to its new home.

55 The correct way to hold a guinea pig is to grasp it around its shoulders with one hand, while using your other hand to support its rear end.

54 If you already have other guinea pigs, it is not difficult to introduce a

56 Guinea pigs do well on the complete diet foods available in flaked and pellet forms at pet stores.

57 Your guinea pig should always have hay to eat, too. The best kind is soft grass hay, rather than the coarser types of hay.

58 You and a guinea pig have something in common. Neither of you can make Vitamin C in your own bodies. Vitamin C is very important. Without it, you could develop a serious disease called **scurvy**.

59 People get their Vitamin C by eating fresh fruits and vegetables. Guinea pigs also need these foods.

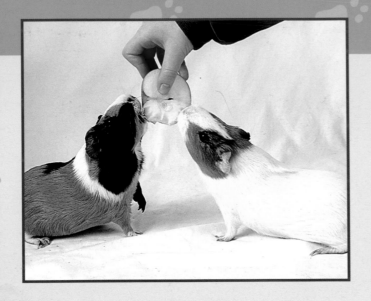

60 Some of the fresh foods guinea pigs like are cauliflower, broccoli, carrots, apples, and oranges.

61 Guinea pigs also like many plants that grow wild or that you might grow in a garden. Dandelion leaves, clover, watercress, marigolds, nasturtiums, and daisies are some favorites.

62 Guinea pigs love lettuce, but too much of it, especially iceberg lettuce, can cause stomach problems. Too much cabbage can cause some of the same kinds of health problems.

63 If you see your pet guinea pig eating its own droppings, do not think it has a bad habit. A guinea pig's soft droppings contain valuable proteins and help it get the full value of its food.

66 Guinea pigs "talk" to each other and make sounds when they are happy, when they are scared, and when they are warning other guinea pigs of danger. As you get to know your pet, you will understand what some of its sounds mean.

64 Feed your guinea pig two meals a day. In the morning, give it a complete diet food and hay. In the evening, give it fresh fruits and vegetables and more hay.

67 Cooing is a sign that all is well. A mother guinea pig will often coo to her babies. If you and your guinea pig become very good friends, it might coo to you.

65 Hand-feeding your pet will help make it more tame.

68 Little squeaks often mean "feed me." High-pitched squeals mean fear, danger, or pain.

69 Chattering teeth mean "stay away." This sound can be a warning to people, as well as other guinea pigs, so watch out! When it clicks its teeth, your guinea pig might bite.

70 When a guinea pig is very happy, it will make a gurgling sound. You might hear gurgles when you give your pet special foods or when an old friend returns to the colony, or even when it is just pleased to see you!

71 To attract females, male guinea pigs make a low, purring sound deep in their throats.

22

75 When a guinea pig lies stretched out, it is relaxed and content. If it sees an enemy, it might "play dead," lying completely still on its back. A sudden sound or movement might make it scatter, or run around wildly.

72 Guinea pigs can see colors.

73 With their large eyes on the sides of their heads, they also can see well to the side and to the back.

76 Friendly guinea pigs, especially members of the same group, touch noses with each other.

74 Your guinea pig's body language can tell you how it is feeling.

23

77 When a guinea pig, usually a female, stands very tall with its legs stiff, it is looking for a fight.

78 Jumping straight up in the air is a special guinea pig habit. The guinea pig is "popcorn jumping," or jumping for joy.

79 A guinea pig needs a clean place to live. You will have to clean your pet's hutch or cage every day – or every other day if your guinea pig spends a lot of time in an exercise run.

80 The daily cleaning should include removing droppings and wet bedding, cleaning food bowls, and filling the water bottle. Moving your guinea pig to an exercise run will make cleaning its hutch or cage much easier.

81 Once a week, you should remove all of the bedding and replace it with fresh bedding material.

84 Smooth-haired breeds should be brushed at least once each week. Breeds with rough coats that have whorls and rosettes need to be brushed every day.

82 Once a month, you should clean the hutch or cage thoroughly. Most pet stores sell a mild **disinfectant** that is safe to use around animals.

83 Grooming your guinea pig is very important, too. You can start brushing your pet as soon as it is settled in its new home.

25

85 Grooming a long-haired Peruvian (above) calls for an expert. Its spectacular coat needs constant attention. The hair on this show breed animal can be almost 20 inches (50 cm) long and needs special care and protection.

86 A Peruvian is born with a short coat that has two rosettes on the rear end. The hair behind the rosettes grows downward. The hair in front of them grows toward the ears.

87 Your guinea pig will not need a bath unless it has been in mud or it has had **diarrhea**. If you need to bathe your pet, you can use baby shampoo, but do not get any lather or soap close to its face.

88 A guinea pig's teeth never stop growing. Sometimes they grow out of line and do not wear down naturally by gnawing. If your guinea pig drools or is having trouble eating its food, it might need to have its teeth clipped by a veterinarian.

89 Your guinea pig might also need to have its toenails clipped, especially if its hutch or cage has soft bedding. To avoid injuring your pet's toes, have a guinea pig expert or a veterinarian do the clipping.

90 If you will be away for a while, ask another guinea pig owner to take care of your pets every day, both in the morning and in the evening. You could also look for a pet store that offers **boarding** services.

92 A guinea pig can be a difficult patient for a veterinarian to treat because it cannot have many of the medicines that can be given to other small animals.

91 With good care, the right foods, and a clean place to live, your pet guinea pig should stay very healthy. Still, you should watch for these signs of illness:

- runny eyes or nose
- drooling
- difficulty eating
- a loss of appetite
- drinking more – or less
- diarrhea
- a matted or dirty coat
- heavy or noisy breathing

93 A female guinea pig can have babies when she is 12 weeks old.

94 Each litter, or group of babies, usually has two to four piglets.

95 The largest litter of guinea pigs on record had 12 piglets – born in a laboratory in 1972.

96 Piglets are born about 63 days after their parents mate.

97 In the wild, guinea pigs are born on open ground, instead of in burrows, so piglets must take care of themselves right from the start.

98 Fortunately, newborn piglets are not very small. Each piglet weighs about 3 ounces (85 g).

99 Newborn piglets also have teeth and a full coat of fur, and their eyes are open.

100 At first, piglets drink only their mother's milk, but in a few days, they can eat solid food.

101 Guinea pigs are great pets – but watch out! You could soon have a houseful!

Glossary

blaze: a white or light-colored stripe running from the forehead to the nose on an animal's face.

boarding: temporary living away from home in a place that provides meals and other care.

breeds: particular types of animals that have been bred within a certain species of animal.

cavies: South American rodents with short tails and rough hair.

crossbred: having parents that are each a different breed.

diarrhea: watery bowel movements that happen too often.

discharge: a thick or watery fluid that seeps through an opening.

disinfectant: a substance that kills disease germs on the surfaces of things.

gnaw: bite steadily on something and wear it away bit by bit.

hutch: an outdoor pen or cage for a small animal, such as a rabbit or a guinea pig.

Incas: the ancient Indian people of Peru in South America.

purebred: having parents that are both the same breed.

rodent: a small mammal with sharp front teeth that never stop growing and must be worn down by gnawing.

scales: small, thin pieces of loose, dry skin.

scurvy: a deadly disease that weakens blood vessels, causing bleeding into the body's tissues.

veterinarian: a doctor who takes care of sick and injured animals.

More Books to Read

Guinea Pigs (First Pets series)
Kate Petty and George Thompson
(Barron's Juveniles)

Guinea Pigs (Nature Watch series) Elvig Hansen
(Carolrhoda Books)

I Love Guinea Pigs (Read and Wonder series) Dick King-Smith
(Candlewick Press)

My Guinea Pig (Welcome Books: My Pets series) Sarah Hughes
(Children's Press)

Web Sites

Caring for Your Guinea Pig
www.petclubhouse.com/
guineapig/5033.htm

Guinea Pig Tele Vision: Almost Live!
www.olywa.net/jandrews

Raising a Healthy Guinea Pig
www.caviesgalore.com/
guinealynx/healthycavy.html

The Rodent Roundup
www.ambleside.schoolzone.co.uk/
ambleweb/rodent/

To find additional web sites, use a reliable search engine, such as www.yahooligans.com, with one or more of the following keywords: **cavies, guinea pigs, rodents**.

Index